C.S.I
TRAIL OF BLOOD

Darlene Stille

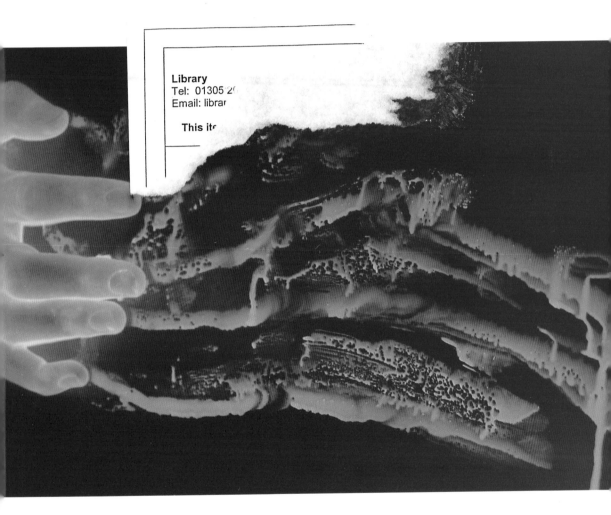

CLASH

by ticktock

Copyright © ticktock Entertainment Ltd 2008

First published in Great Britain in 2008 by ticktock Media Ltd,
2 Orchard Business Centre, North Farm Road, Tunbridge Wells, Kent, TN2 3XF

ticktock project editor: Ruth Owen
ticktock project designer: Sara Greasley
ticktock picture researcher: Lizzie Knowles

**With thanks to series editors Honor Head and Jean Coppendale,
and consultant John Cassella, Principal Lecturer in Forensic Science, Staffordshire University, UK**

Thank you to Lorraine Petersen and the members of *nasen*

ISBN 978 1 84696 720 7 pbk

Printed in China

A CIP catalogue record for this book is available from the British Library.

Picture credits (t=top; b=bottom; c=centre; l=left; r=right):
BioPhoto Associate/ Science Photo Library: 17. Mauro Fermariello/ Science Photo Library: 7. Pablo Paul/ Alamy: 8t,
10b. Photodisc/ Photolibrary: OFC. Philippe Psaila/ Science Photo Library: 9. Revy, ISM/ Science Photo Library: 19.
Alexis Rosenfeld/ Science Photo Library: 24-25. Shutterstock: OFC background, 1, 2-3, 4, 5, 6, 11, 12, 14-15, 16t, 18,
20, 26-27b, 28, 29, 31. Volker Steger, Peter Arnold Inc/ Science Photo Library: 10t. Andrew Syred/ Science Photo
Library 16b. Tek Image/ Science Photo Library: 8b, 22-23. Hayley Terry: 27t. Geoff Tompkinson/ Science Photo
Library: 21. Jim Varney/ Science Photo Library: 13.

Every effort has been made to trace copyright holders, and we apologise in advance for any omissions. We would be
pleased to insert the appropriate acknowledgments in any subsequent edition of this publication.

Contents

A 23-year-old man has gone missing.
He was last seen two weeks ago at work.

There is no sign of a break-in or fight at his flat.
His clothes, suitcase and passport are in the flat.

All the rooms are very clean.
There are no towels or tissues in the bathroom.

The flat looks too clean...

...could it be a crime scene?

The police think a crime has been committed.
They have two suspects.

Suspect A

The man's ex-girlfriend.
They argued before he went missing.

Suspect B

The man's flatmate.
The police find out
the flatmate owes the
man thousands of
pounds. The flatmate
cannot be found.

CHAPTER 2

AT THE CRIME SCENE

The police want to find out if a crime has been committed.

The police put crime scene tape around the man's home. They send for the crime scene investigators (CSIs).

CSIs look for evidence at a crime scene. They look for evidence such as blood, fingerprints and hairs.

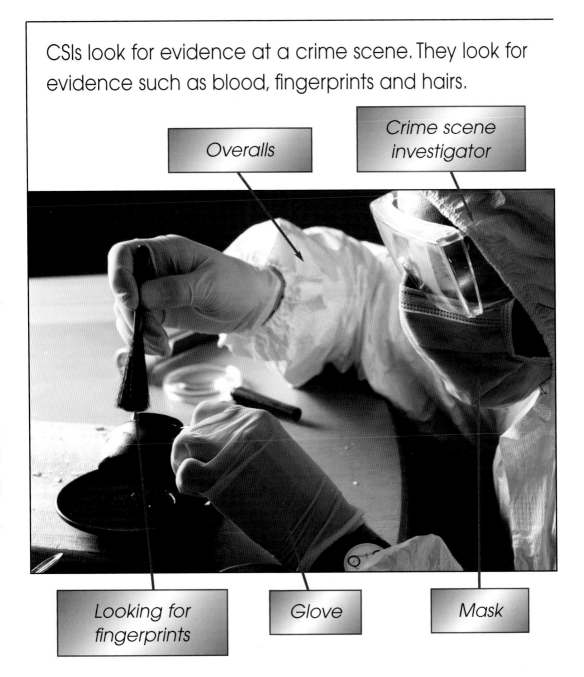

Overalls

Crime scene investigator

Looking for fingerprints

Glove

Mask

The CSIs wear gloves, masks, shoe covers and white overalls. The overalls and gloves stop the CSIs leaving their own hairs or fingerprints at the crime scene.

They must keep any evidence clean.

The crime scene investigators search the flat. They look at everything.

Markers

They take photographs and make videos.
They put markers where they find evidence.

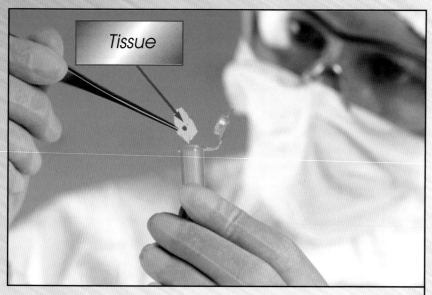

Tissue

They find a tiny piece of tissue. It looks as if there is dried blood on the tissue.

The CSI does a chemical test on the piece of tissue.

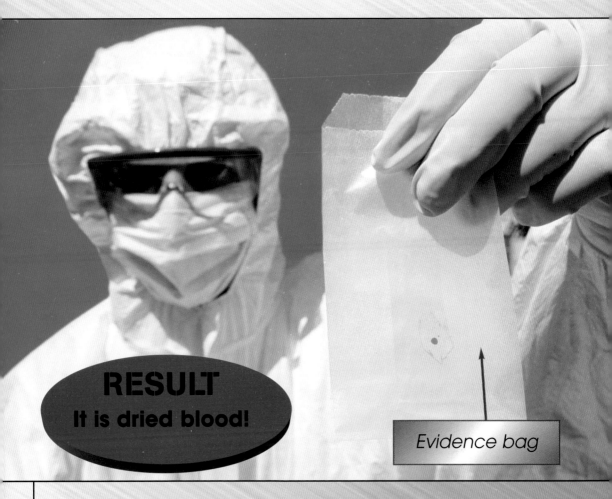

RESULT
It is dried blood!

Evidence bag

The piece of tissue is put into an evidence bag.
Then it is taken to the crime lab.

NEED TO KNOW

Blood starts to dry after three to five minutes.
Wet blood is better than dried blood for testing.
Wet blood can show if the person was taking drugs
or drinking alcohol.

CSIs can collect blood from a crime scene in different ways.

They can use tape to pick up bits of dried blood.

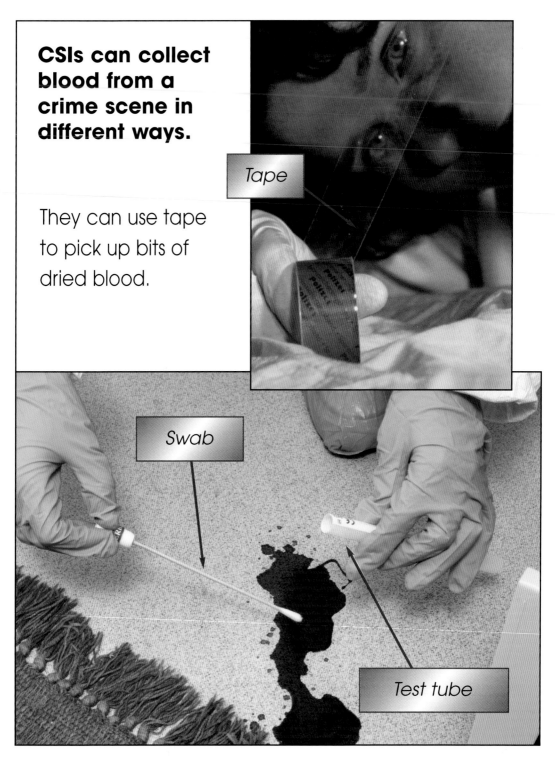

Tape

Swab

Test tube

CSIs can collect wet blood with a swab. Then they seal it in a test tube.

When a person is injured, blood from their wounds makes patterns, or spatters.

Blood on a wall can tell a forensic scientist how high a wound was. It can also tell the scientist if the wounded person was standing or sitting.

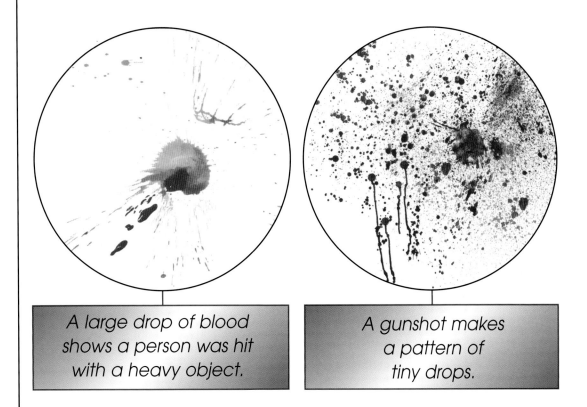

A large drop of blood shows a person was hit with a heavy object.

A gunshot makes a pattern of tiny drops.

Scientists can tell what sort of weapon caused a wound by looking at the size of the blood drops.

They study the shape of the drops made by a gunshot to work out the angle of the bullet.

The CSIs search the missing man's flat.
They cannot find bloodstains or blood
spatters in any rooms.

Has the crime scene been cleaned?

It doesn't matter how well a murderer scrubs a crime scene, the CSIs can find hidden bloodstains.

The bath looks really clean. But is it?

The CSIs rub a swab over an area of the bath to see if there are any hidden traces of blood.

Next, the swab is dabbed onto a piece of damp filter paper. Special chemicals are put on to the filter paper.

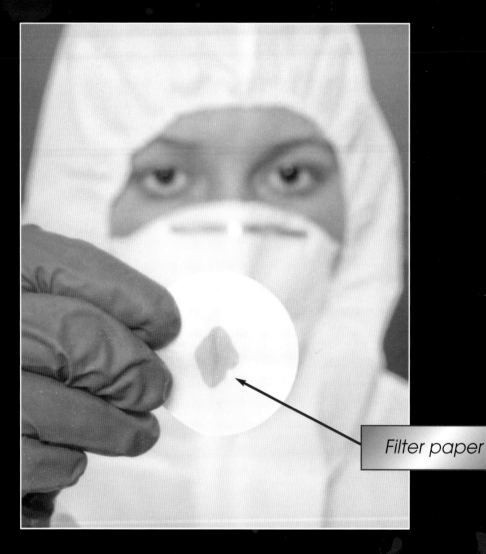

Filter paper

The filter paper turns purple. This means there is blood on the bath. The filter paper is taken to the lab for testing.

The CSIs find hidden blood in the hallway, too!

Was the man stabbed in his bathroom?

Was his body dragged from the flat?

Has there been a murder?

CHAPTER 3

AT THE CRIME LAB

The piece of tissue and the filter paper are taken to the crime lab.

Forensic scientist

A forensic scientist analyses the two blood samples.

The scientist tests the blood to find out if it is from a man or a woman.

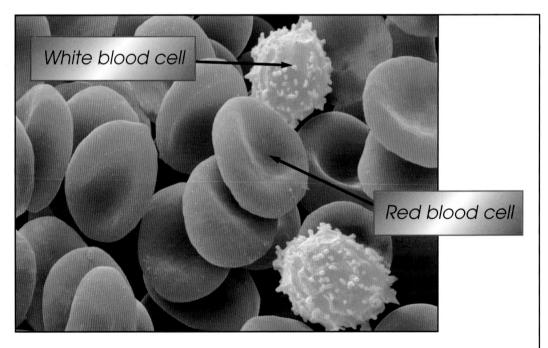

White blood cell

Red blood cell

Blood is made up of cells. Each white cell has a part called a nucleus.

A human nucleus contains two chromosomes.
There are X and Y chromosomes.

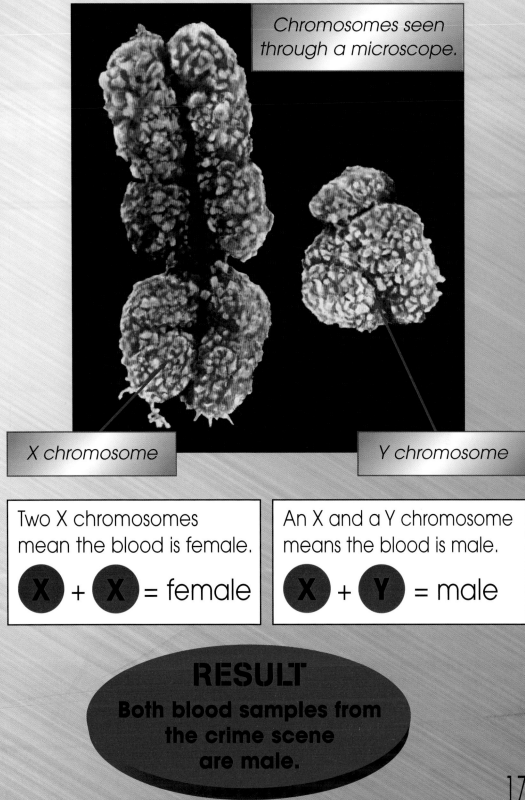

Chromosomes seen through a microscope.

X chromosome

Y chromosome

Two X chromosomes mean the blood is female.

X + **X** = female

An X and a Y chromosome means the blood is male.

X + **Y** = male

RESULT

Both blood samples from the crime scene are male.

Next, the forensic scientist tests the blood to find out what blood type it is.

There are four different types of human blood.

The types are A, B, AB and O.

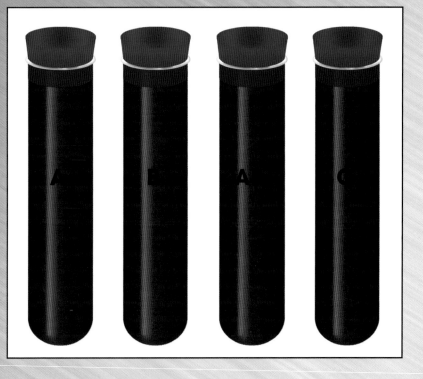

All humans are one of these four blood types.

The forensic scientist uses chemicals to test the blood samples from the crime scene.

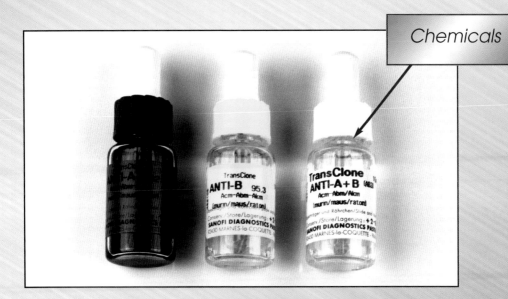

Different blood types react in different ways to the chemicals. This shows the scientists what blood type a sample is.

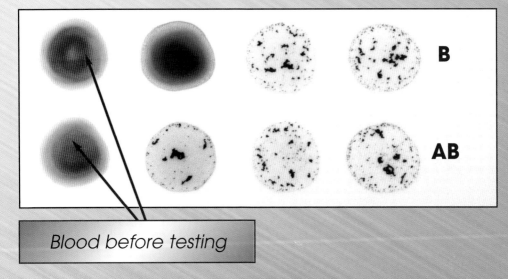

B

AB

Blood before testing

RESULT

One blood sample is type B and one sample is type AB.

Forensic scientists can also check the blood samples for another important clue – DNA.

Cells in our body are unique.

They contain unique information called DNA.

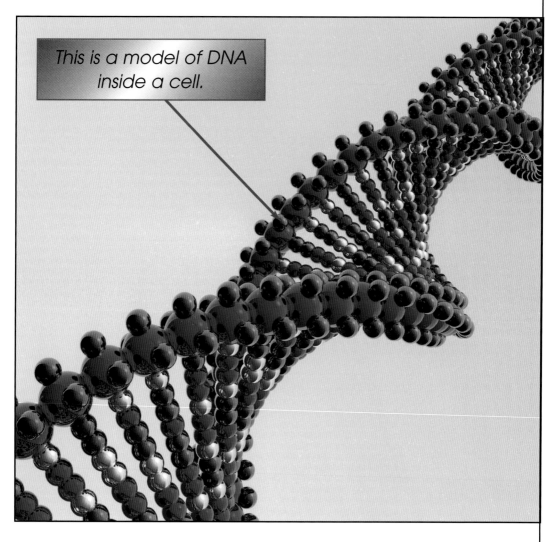

This is a model of DNA inside a cell.

Only identical twins have the same DNA.

DNA tests are done on the two blood samples from the crime scene.

A special machine 'reads' the DNA.
The machine displays the information
in a pattern called a DNA profile.

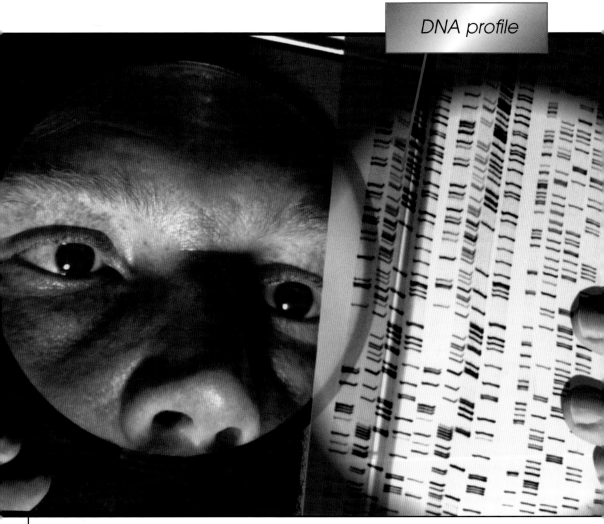

DNA profile

A DNA profile is unique. The police can match it to
a profile from a suspect or from a victim.

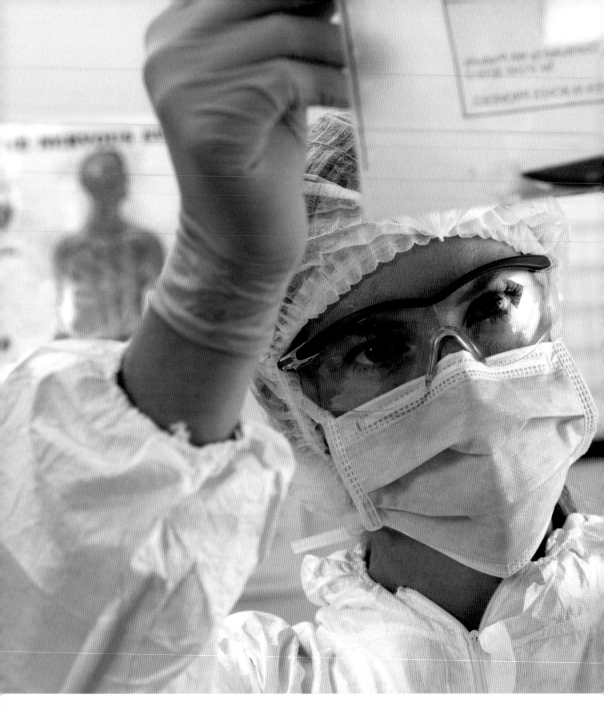

The police search the ex-girlfriend's house. In the garden they find a bloody knife.

The forensic scientists find two different samples of blood on the knife.

RESULT
Both blood samples are male;
one is type O, one is type AB;
the DNA profiles of the blood on
the suit match the profiles from
the crime scene.

CHAPTER 4

A BREAKTHROUGH

The ex-girlfriend is the number one suspect.

She had a motive. She was angry about the break-up.
A knife covered in human blood was found in her garden.

Police diver

The ex-girlfriend says she is innocent.
She says the knife was planted by the flatmate.
She says the flatmate is trying to frame her.
The police need more evidence.

Then there is a breakthrough!

A diver finds a man's body in a lake.
Police divers recover the body from the lake.

Body

**The man's body is taken to the crime lab.
There are stab wounds on the body.
It is the missing man!**

The man's body was floating face down in
the lake. It was held down with heavy stones.
But, there is blood clotted on the man's back.

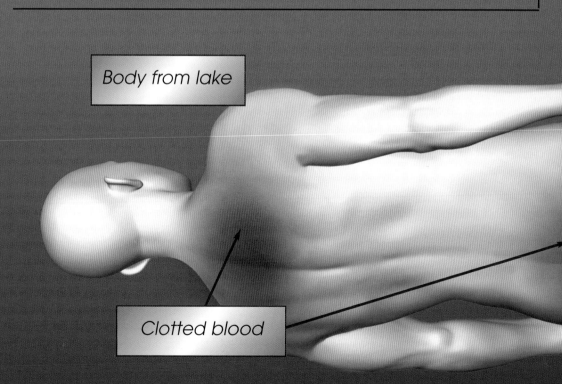

Body from lake

Clotted blood

Blood stops flowing when the heart stops beating. Gravity pulls blood to the body parts closest to the ground. The blood clots and stays there.

Could this mean that the man was on his back when he died?

Was his body then moved to the lake?

This blood evidence can sometimes help the police piece together what happened in a murder case.

The forensic scientists run blood tests on the body.

RESULT
The man's blood is type AB.
His DNA matches the blood in a blood sample from the bath and the knife.

27

CHAPTER 5

THE CHARGE

The police think the man was stabbed in his flat. Then his body was dumped in the lake. But who committed the crime?

The ex-girlfriend

The police question the ex-girlfriend again. She breaks down and confesses.

She says the flatmate committed the crime and she helped him. But then the flatmate got scared. She says he hid the knife in her garden to frame her.

She says the flatmate cut himself on the knife during the attack.

The flatmate

The police find and arrest the flatmate.

The flatmate says he is innocent. He says the ex-girlfriend hates him and is trying to frame him.

He says he was out of town. He has never seen the knife.

The police test the flatmate's blood and make a DNA profile.

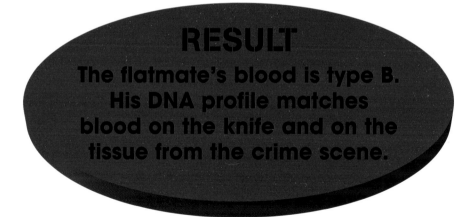

RESULT

The flatmate's blood is type B. His DNA profile matches blood on the knife and on the tissue from the crime scene.

The ex-girlfriend and the flatmate are both charged with murder.

CASE SOLVED!

NEED TO KNOW WORDS

cell The smallest living unit of a plant or animal. Body tissue and organs are made up of many cells.

chromosome A structure in the nucleus of cells that carries DNA.

clot To thicken from a liquid into a solid.

crime lab A laboratory with equipment that is used for scientific experiments and tests on crime scene evidence.

crime scene Any place where a crime has happened. A crime scene can be a house, a car or even a field.

crime scene investigator (CSI) A person who examines crime scenes and collects evidence.

DNA The special code in the centre (or nucleus) of each person's cells. Our DNA makes us all unique.

evidence Facts and signs that can show what happened during a crime.

forensic scientist An expert who examines detailed information from a crime scene and analyses it to work out what happened.

frame To make a false accusation so that an innocent person looks guilty.

gravity A force that pulls everything down towards the ground.

innocent Free from guilt or blame.

motive A reason for committing a crime.

nucleus The centre part of a cell that contains the DNA.

suspect A person who is thought to have carried out a crime.

victim A person who is hurt or killed.

NEED TO KNOW FACTS

- **Collecting DNA**
  DNA can be collected from blood, skin, hair and nails. It can even be collected from sweat and spit.

- **Blood fact**
  Most adults have about 4.7 litres of blood in their body.

- **Blood types fact**
  Doctors tried for many years to transfuse blood from one person to another. Sometimes the blood went lumpy and the person died. In 1901, a scientist named Karl Landsteiner discovered the four blood types. A blood transfusion only works if a person is given the right type of blood.

- **Blood transfusions**
  Today, many adults donate (give) blood. It is stored in bags in hospitals. If a person loses blood, it can be replaced by donated blood in a blood transfusion.

CRIME ONLINE

WEBSITES

www.pbs.org/wnet/redgold/journey/index.html
Find out what blood does inside your body

www.centredessciencesdemontreal.com/en/jeunes/jeunes_jeux.htm
Collect and analyse clues to find out who committed a murder

http://www.fbi.gov/kids/6th12th/6th12th.htm
How the FBI investigates crimes

http://www.howstuffworks.com/csi5.htm
All about the world of CSI

INDEX